THE SAGA OF THE
JÓMSVÍKINGS

THE SAGA OF THE
JÓMSVÍKINGS

*Translated from the Old Icelandic
with Introduction and Notes by*

Lee M. Hollander

Illustrated by Malcolm Thurgood

UNIVERSITY OF TEXAS PRESS   AUSTIN

International Standard Book Number 0-292-77623-3
Library of Congress Catalog Card Number 54-7338
Copyright © 1955 by the University of Texas Press
All rights reserved
Printed in the United States of America

Second Paperback Printing, 1990

Requests for permission to reproduce material from this work should be sent to Permissions,
University of Texas Press, Box 7819, Austin, Texas 78713-7819.

∞The paper used in this publication meets the minimum requirements of American National
Standard for Information Sciences—Permanence of Paper for Printed Library Materials, ANSI
Z39.48-1984.

TO MY NORWEGIAN FRIENDS

FOREWORD

IT IS DIFFICULT, if not impossible, to achieve consistency in the rendering of Old Norse names. I have substituted the English equivalents wherever possible but have left the original forms of others. Pronunciation of names should present little difficulty if the reader will bear in mind that the acute accent over a vowel indicates length of the vowel (all not so marked being short) and that vowels have the Continental values. "Ey" may be pronounced like the English long "i." The "g" is always hard, and "j" is like the "y" in "yes." Most importantly, *stress invariably falls on a first syllable.*

I have endeavored to make the translation conform as closely to the original text as is compatible with English idiom, and, while furnishing such information as seemed necessary for the proper understanding of the text, to refrain from overloading the pages with annotations. In a few instances words in brackets have been supplied for obvious lacunae.

L. M. H.

CONTENTS

· 11

INTRODUCTION

THE GREAT NAVAL BATTLE in Hjórunga Bay (A.D. 986) in which Earl Hákon, ruler of most of Norway, crushed an invading fleet of Danes left a lasting impression on the imagination of Icelandic storytellers. No fewer than five Icelandic skalds took part in it under the Norwegian banner. On their homecoming, no doubt they regaled news-hungry compatriots with accounts of the battle; and in their verses they have left us contemporary reflections of the event.

Two centuries later there appeared a saga (in several versions) about the Jómsvíkings, the members of the warrior community constituting the invaders. Though it is generally classed as one of the historical sagas and though its matter has to do with events involving the fate of nations, even a superficial consideration of its structure and content shows that it is what we would to-day call a historical novel rather than a history. We find that the kernel of historic truth about the battle and the events leading up to it has been encrusted with accretions of more or less fanciful details.

The earmarks of deliberate composition are plain. Indeed, this saga furnishes an instructive example of how historical fact is transmuted into legend: practically all of the main characters are historic, but the details of their actions and speeches, though related soberly enough, are either pure inventions or variations of folk traditions that had grown up about the incidents. This aura of invention is particularly apparent in the first part of the story— a part lacking in one of the redactions—but to a lesser degree can be sensed throughout the whole tale.

Thus it hardly needs to be pointed out to the attentive reader how prominent, and effective, a role is assigned to the retarding epic device of the threefold repetition that is so characteristic of legend and lore. King Gorm has three dreams about the hard times to befall Denmark, forestalled then by the wise counsel of his queen. The three marvels portending coming events that stop Earl Klak-Harold at the Lim Firth are interpreted satisfactorily by him to the king. Palnatóki comes only on the third summons to take part in the funeral feast for King Harold. Three times a hostile invasion is prevented by the resourcefulness of a prince's daughter or wife—itself a legendary motif. A telling crescendo is effected by the young Svein's threefold and ever more impudent appearance before his reputed father to push his claims, each appearance followed by a more cruel harrying of the king's subjects. Even the three successive arrivals of Sigvaldi, Búi, and Vagn at the gate of Jómsborg show elements of this favorite device of the storyteller, as do the quarrels between Véseti and Strút-Harold, with the threefold reprisals following. Earl Hákon must call three times on his tutelary goddess Thorgerd before obtaining her assistance; and the course of the battle itself is broken into three phases by his repeated invocation of the demoness and her sister.

Legendary traits bulk especially in the first part. In the very first chapter the story of Knút's origin from the incestuous union of brother and sister, and of his exposure, finding, and adoption by the king has the characteristics of folklore and is reminiscent of many tales—those for instance of King Helgi Kraki, famous in legend, of Sinfjotli, the son and nephew of Sigmund, and particularly so, of the birth, exposure, finding, and upbringing of Moses (who according to some medieval legends was born in incestuous union). Again, the dreams of Gorm and their interpretation by Thýra recall the dreams of Pharaoh as interpreted by Joseph and the measures taken to ward off the coming famine. Ingeborg's dream of the web weighted with human heads definitely recalls the famous "Song of the Valkyries."

Later on in the story we can detect a novelistic and stereotype motif in the stratagem used both by Palnatóki (when attending King Harold's funeral feast) and by Sigvaldi (in enticing King Svein aboard his ship): each man has the prows of his fleet pointing away from land for a quick getaway. The parallelism between the families of Véseti and Strút-Harold, in that each has two warlike sons and one marriageable daughter, is another stereotype. The supernatural comes in only once—disregarding the quasi-historical Christian ordeal of Bishop Poppo (not occurring in the version chosen for our translation)—to wit, in the magic storm superinduced by Earl Hákon's sacrifice of his youngest son. And, strange to say, this occurrence has far more authenticity, so far as tradition goes, than any of the other legendary elements. Even the skeptical historian Snorri mentions the hailstorm, a rather unusual phenomenon in western Norway, as a decisive incident in turning the tide of battle, though to be sure he does not ascribe it to a supernatural agency.

In general, and typical of tales of the legendary type, the multiplicity and complexity, as well as the contemporaneity, of historical events are here reduced to simplicity and sequency.

It stands to reason that the fairly copious speeches, which dramatically enliven and at the same time advance the action, are the property of the author—barring the exchange between old King Gorm and his queen, which has the air of a reminiscence of some lost lay, the words of the Jómsvíkings at Túnsberg addressed to Vagn, which have an authentic ring, and the remarks of the Icelandic skalds present at the various stages of the conflict, which may be considered as contemporary reporting.

This is not the place to go into extensive detail about where and how far the saga deviates from what we now know to have been historical fact. For one thing, we have learned to regard, and value, the sagas—apart from the critical works of writers like Snorri, Ari, Abbot Karl Jónsson—not so much as reliable historical documents but as art products making only a secondary claim on historical veracity. Nevertheless it is well to realize that in some important aspects (as well as in innumerable small points) our saga is conspicuously at variance with the facts.

Let us note principally that, in the interest of heightening the contrast between King Harold and his calm, deeply planning antagonist Palnatóki, serious injustice is done to Harold (Blacktooth, died *ca.* 985) in depicting him as an irascible, mediocre, and licentious man, weakly envious of his powerful vassals. In history he stands as a strong and capable ruler. According to the evidence of the larger Runestone of Jellinge, erected by Harold in memory of his father Gorm and his mother Thýra, it was he who united Denmark and "made the Danes Christians," long before Emperor Otto's expedition (which, by the way, was in retaliation for a Danish raid, and not to convert the Danes). The whole web of intrigue and violence through which, according to the saga, he is supposed to have rid himself (in connivance with Earl Hákon) of Harold Grayfur of Norway, Harold's mother, Queen Gunnhild, and finally of his own nephew, Gold-Harold, is inconsistent with his historical character and apparently more fiction than fact. And it was not a mythical Palnatóki but Harold who founded the warrior community of the Jómsvíkings (as a bulwark against the Wends); its members remained loyal to him and actually aided him in his fight against his rebellious son, Svein. In fact, the dominating figure of Palnatóki and his character and exploits, though possibly based on a compound of certain Tell-like legends and perhaps local Danish tradition, must be wholly credited to the inventive genius of the author.

The saga also does less than justice to King Svein (Forkbeard), historically an energetic and popular ruler: the conquest by him of most of England (1013) would not have been possible if he had not had the lasting support of the majority of his people. The attack on Norway by the Jómsvíkings, aided and abetted by him, was in all probability not merely a scheme to avenge himself on them for having captured him and transported him to Jómsborg but part of a grand plan to subject all northern lands to Danish rule—a plan which his son Knút (Canute the Great), long sovereign of Denmark, England, and Norway, came near carrying out.

On the other hand the author's portrayal of Earl Hákon's character essentially tallies with the facts. Though in true saga style the narrator never shows his hand, yet we are made to feel a certain amount of admiration for that ruthless and immensely resourceful worshiper of the ancient gods, heathen Norway's last great figure, who did indeed win the loving admiration of his fellow-countrymen and who was hailed by them as their deliverer from the Danish yoke (see note 54, page 94). No lesser man than Ólaf Tryggvason, the hero king of Norway, is brought in by the author as foil and ally of Emperor Otto in order to offset Earl Hákon's generalship— a semifictional touch, for actually Ólaf was a mere stripling when the German hosts broke through the Dannevirke (*ca.* 975) and was not to become the earl's great antagonist until years later.

The saga is told in a—deceptively—simple style, with now and then a deft touch of irony. There are no sur-

mises as to the identity of the author. His Icelandic pro-
venience is obvious from the entirely episodic interest he
takes in the presence and doings of the Icelandic skalds
who participated in the great battle. His knowledge of
the complicated Danish littoral is vague, but he becomes
more precise with the approach of the Danish fleet to
Norway, a country whose geography every traveled Ice-
lander knew almost as well as that of his own. If he did
have a clerical training—indications of which might be
seen in the clerically tinged dreams of King Gorm and
the visions of Earl Klak-Harold—he certainly is not
overly enthusiastic about the Christianity which, according to him, was rammed down the throats of the Danes
by Emperor Otto. Nor does he show much pious indig-
nation at Earl Hákon's apostasy and rank heathen prac-
tices.* The old heroic ideal of uninhibited and unabashed
self-assertion and the martial virtues appeal to him far
more than Christian ethics—of which, in sober truth,
there is no trace in the saga. One senses his unconcealed
admiration for figures such as the manly, forthright Búi

* It is for this reason, among others, that the short version of Codex
Holmiensis 7, quarto, seems more authentic than, as well as aestheti-
cally superior to, the watered-down other versions which, quite un-
organically and against the *spirit* of the saga, bring in the miracle of
Bishop Poppo (whose successful undergoing of the ordeal is said to
have convinced the Danes of the superiority of the new faith) and
which speak of Hákon's human sacrifice with vigorous condemnation.

and the audacious, dashing Vagn. He is at his best when he tells of fierce fighting or crafty stratagem.

He is superb in the "Testing of the Jómsvíkings" (Chap. 23), where he gives us men who know how to die. They look death unflinchingly in the eye and with a jest on their lips. They love life but would not be able to survive the taunt of having begged for it. It is as though they were conceived as embodiments and ensamples of the noble sentiment of the Eddic "Hávamól" (stanza 77).*

> Cattle die   and kinsmen die,
>   thyself eke soon wilt die;
> but fair fame   will fade never,
>   I ween, for him who wins it.

It would be difficult to cite in world literature a parallel to that unforgettable scene. Though it was no doubt based on a modicum of tradition, possibly even a grain of historic truth—the incredible marriage of Vagn with the daughter of his would-be slayer must have caused comment and invited elaboration—yet in its present, expanded form it is beyond peradventure a product of the narrative genius of the author. Who knows but that it was conceived as a kind of apotheosis of the unconquer-

* See "The Sayings of Hór" in *The Poetic Edda,* tr. Lee M. Hollander (The University of Texas, 1928).

able heroism of the Viking Age—to the author a fabled, glorious past—a heroism which dwarfed the "heroics" of the southern romances which were becoming fashionable about the time the saga was written; or perhaps as a telling contrast to the unprincipled savagery of the Sturlung period, in which the author lived.

The family sagas present us with a wealth of sharply etched and individualized portraits; but this author, in consonance with the highly fictive nature of his work, gives us characters which are types rather than individuals. Thus Búi, Vagn, Sigvaldi are all seen in the one plane of their dominant traits—manly intrepidity, reckless heroism, foxy shrewdness, respectively. Only one character may be said to exemplify all the ideals of heathen Norse antiquity: Palnatóki, warrior and born leader, founder and kingmaker. But contrary to most of the purely fictitious sagas of the North, and in agreement here with the cool objectivity of the family sagas, there is no one "hero" around whom events are centered and whose part we take. Our sympathies are not exclusively engaged on one side, even in the great battle, but veer now to the one, now to the other.

Reacting to earlier implicit belief in the historic reliability of the sagas, modern historians have occasionally gone to the other extreme. Thus, in the case of this saga, one highly respected scholar has even doubted the presence of the Jómsvíkings in the battle. However, a close study of contemporary skaldic verse bearing on the matter and a consideration of the general harmony between the diverse redactions of the saga on this score decisively confute the doubt.

Again, some scholars contend that the first part of the saga—dealing with the origins of the Knytling dynasty, the attack by Emperor Otto, and Earl Hákon's apostasy and refusal to stay tributary to Denmark—is a later addition. Here a comparison with the usual technique of the sagas in the matter of dreams and prognostications inclines one to the belief that on the contrary this part was well planned as integrated preparation for what follows in the second part: the son born in incest heralds the later greatness of the royal line; the dreams of Gorm the Old are preparatory to his queen's constructive activity; Earl Klak-Harold's visions presage not only the introduction of Christianity under King Harold but the coming dissensions and deeds of treachery to ensue in the royal house; and, finally, the maneuvers of Earl Hákon for achieving independence explain why the astute Svein is more than willing to aid the Jómsvíkings in their desperate adventure. It is all well thought out. These considerations are supported, moreover, by the fact that the two parts do not differ markedly in vocabulary, style, or mode of attack, aside from the preponderance of the purely legendary in the first part, which is, after all, a feature found also in the earlier portions of some family sagas whose organic unity is not questioned.

As to the various redactions in which the saga has come down to us, differing as they do in innumerable details but also agreeing verbally in ever so many others, the only reasonable assumption is that once the story was put together by the original author other reciters of it, in sovereign free fashion, added, embellished, diluted, condensed wherever they saw fit, and to such an extent that it is well-nigh hopeless to say with any degree of assurance that this or that redaction represents an earlier or a later form. At any rate, for translation the short version of Codex Holmiensis 7, quarto (in the Royal Library in Stockholm), is by all odds preferable, and has therefore been used.

Ever since this saga of derring-do became accessible to the Scandinavians, early in the nineteenth century, it has been a favorite with them. The great Romantic poets of Denmark, Oehlenschläger and N. F. S. Grundt-vig, have treated certain portions of it in noble poems: it may be doubted if the story as a whole will ever be better told. It has not attracted the attention of writers in the English-speaking world—understandably so, since there exists no readily accessible English translation. Certain difficulties in the text, hesitation as to the choice of redaction, and perhaps the thoroughly heathen character of the tale may have been deterrent. The only available English version known to the present writer is the romanticized and rather Victorian treatment of the material by Sir George Webbe Dasent in *The Vikings of the Baltic*, published in three volumes in 1875.

THE SAGA *of the* JÓMSVÍKINGS

1. KNŮT THE FOUNDLING

GORM[1] WAS THE NAME of a king who ruled over Denmark and was called the Childless. He was a mighty king, and popular with his subjects. He had long governed his kingdom when the events to be told happened. At that time there was in Saxland[2] an earl called Arnfinn, who held his land in fief from King Charlemagne. Arn-

---

[1] The name is in all likelihood a contraction from *Guthorm*—"reverer of the gods."

[2] The Old Norse name for Germany, especially the northern portion inhabited by the Saxons.

finn and King Gorm were good friends and had been on viking expeditions together. The earl had a beautiful sister, and he was fonder of her than he should have been and begot a child with her; the child was kept hidden, and then the earl sent men away with it but bade them not to desert it before they knew what would befall it.

They came to Denmark and to a forest. They were aware that King Gorm was in the forest hunting with his followers. They laid the child under a tree and hid themselves.

In the evening the king left the forest, and so did all of his men except two brothers,[3] the one named Hallvard and the other, Hávard—they had tarried behind. [And having lost their way in the darkness] they went on toward the sea. When they heard a child crying they went in that direction, not knowing what it could be. They found there a boy child lying under a tree, and a great cloth was knotted in the branches above him. The child was swathed in garments of costly fabric, and around his head was tied a silken ribbon, and in it, a golden ring weighing an ounce. They took the child up and carried him home with them. And when they returned the king was at table, drinking, and they told the king what they had found and showed him the boy.

[3] The brothers are, of course, to be regarded as purely fictitious.

The king was pleased with him and said: "This boy is likely to be the child of people of great account, and it is well that he was found." And he had the boy child baptized with water and had him called Knút because gold had been knotted in the cloth about his head.[4] The king gave him good foster parents[5] and called him his son and loved him greatly. And when King Gorm grew old he made Knút his foster son heir to his kingdom. Thereupon King Gorm died. Then Knút took possession of all the realm Gorm had ruled, and he came to be

[4] The whole legend evidently had its origin in the (early) popular misunderstanding of the name, which corresponds to the Old High German *chnútz*, "bold," whereas the Old Norse word *knútr* signifies "a knot." The Knytling dynasty of Denmark derives from this ancestral figure. The baptism referred to is the old (heathen) ceremony.

[5] In Scandinavian antiquity a child was commonly given to foster parents to bring up.

loved by the people. He begot one son, whose name was Gorm. He was first called Gorm the Silly, but when he was grown up, Gorm the Old or the Mighty.[6]

2. KING GORM'S DREAMS

HAROLD WAS THE NAME of an earl who ruled over Holtsetaland.[7] He was called Klak-Harold.[8] He was a wise man. The earl had a daughter named Thýra. She had a prophetic gift and was a most beautiful woman and knew how to interpret dreams better than anyone else. The earl loved her dearly, and with her advice considered he had the governance of his people firmly in hand.

[6] On the smaller (and older) Runestone of Jellinge, Gorm is termed "the Improver, or Savior, of Denmark," because of his building, or reinforcing, the Dannevirke—the immemorial line of fortification between the Sli Firth and the Eider River against incursions from the south—and his obtaining sway over all of Denmark. Until recently, owing to an early misunderstanding of the inscription, this appellation was attributed to Queen Thýra, both in legend and history. The stone is a fine example of the *bautasteinar* (grave monuments), rude monoliths erected over the graves of eminent persons.

[7] The present Holstein.

[8] The significance of the first element of this name is uncertain.

30 ·

Now when Gorm had become grown and taken over the rule of his kingdom he left his land with a great following of men, for the purpose of asking the daughter of Earl Harold in marriage; and in case the earl refused to give him his daughter he meant to lay waste his land. When Earl Harold and his daughter learned of King Gorm's coming and his intentions, they sent men to meet him and to invite him to a splendid banquet; and the king accepted that. And when Gorm had made his wishes known to the earl, the earl answered that his daughter was to decide for herself, "because she is much wiser than I."[9] So the king addressed his suit to her.

Thereupon she made answer as follows: "This is not a matter to be decided on immediately. You shall journey home now, with good and worthy gifts from us. But if you are minded to ask me in marriage, when you arrive home you shall have a house built where none stood before, one which is suitable for you to sleep in; and in it you shall sleep the first night of winter, and three nights in a row. And remember clearly what dreams you have, and have your messengers tell me. Then I shall let the messengers know whether you are to come to fetch me in marriage. But if you have no dreams you need not persist."

[9] The unannounced transition from indirect to direct speech, or vice versa, is characteristic of saga style.

The king journeyed home with honorable parting gifts and meant indeed to put her wisdom to the test. And when he arrived in his own land he proceeded as she had told him; then he slept three nights in the house, but had three[10] of his men keep watch about it to prevent any treason against him.

Thereupon the king sent his messengers to the earl and his daughter to tell them his dreams.[11] When she had heard what his dreams were she told the men to say to the king that she would marry him. And the messengers told the king how matters stood, and he was very glad. He quickly outfitted a great company to go with him to fetch home his bride. Then King Gorm arrived in Holtsetaland, and the earl learned of his coming and prepared a great feast for him. And then the marriage was celebrated; and for entertainment at the banquet King Gorm told his dreams and Queen Thýra interpreted them.

The king told how in the first night he dreamed that he was out in the open and looked over all his kingdom. It seemed to him that the sea receded from the land so

[10] Or, as the other versions have it, and more likely, three hundred men.

[11] The gift of interpreting dreams or visions appears to have been a family trait. Earl Klak-Harold has it, and so has his daughter and his granddaughter Ragnhild, who was married to King Halvdan the Black of Norway; see Snorri's *Heimskringla: Halfdana saga Svarta*, chap. 5.

far that he could not reach it with his eyes; and all the sounds and firths were dry. Then he saw three white oxen come up out of the sea. They ate all the grass from off the ground and thereupon went back into the sea.

In the second dream it seemed to him that again three oxen came up out of the sea. They were all red and had great horns. They too ate all the grass from off the ground and then returned into the sea.

And in his third dream the king again saw three oxen come up out of the sea. These were all black of color, and by far the largest and had the greatest horns; and they also ate the grass off the land and thereupon went back into the sea.

And after that he heard a crash so great that he thought it could be heard over all of Denmark, and he saw that it came from the rush of the sea as it returned to the land.

"And now, Queen, I would that you interpret these dreams for the entertainment of our men."

She said that so it should be.

"When you saw the three white oxen come up on land from the sea, that signified that three winters with great snows will come, so that the fruitfulness of the land in Denmark will diminish. When you saw the three red oxen coming up on land, that signified that three winters will come with little snow, and that is not good either. And when there came out of the sea the three oxen which were black, that signified three winters to come so bad that no one can remember the like of them. And so great a famine will befall as never yet within the memory of man. And as to the oxen having big horns, that signified that many a man will be deprived of all he owns. And when in your dream you heard a great crash from the tumult of the sea, that is likely to betoken warfare in this land between men of great might near to you in kin. If you had dreamed the first night as you did the last, then this turmoil of warfare would have occurred in your days, and then I would not have gone with you; but against the famine I can devise some measures."

After this banquet King Gorm and Queen Thýra journeyed back to Denmark. And they had many ships laden with grain and other good things conveyed into Denmark, and so every year thereafter until the famine came. And then they lacked for nothing, nor did anyone who lived in their neighborhood, because the king and queen shared these good things with their countrymen. And Thýra was the wisest woman who ever came to Denmark, and she was called the Savior of Denmark.[12]

King Gorm and Queen Thýra had two sons. The older was called Knút and the younger, Harold. Both were promising men, but Knút was the wiser. He was fos-

[12] See note 6.

tered by Earl Klak-Harold, his maternal grandfather. The earl loved him greatly, and he was dear to many. But Harold, who stayed at home at the court, was very ill liked as a youth.

3. EARL HAROLD'S VISIONS

Now it happened that King Gorm sent messengers to Earl Klak-Harold to invite him to his Yule feast. The earl accepted with pleasure, and the messengers of the king returned. Thereupon the earl made ready for the journey. And when he and his men came to the Lim Firth[13] they saw a strange tree standing before them. This tree bore both small green apples and blossoms. They marveled greatly at that. And the earl said it was a great portent to have happened at this time of the year, because they saw that apples both large and old had

[13] An arm of the sea separating the northernmost portion of Jutland from the mainland. Before the great break-through to the west (1825) it was essentially a collection of fresh-water lakes. Just why the earl wishes to cross this firth is not clear, because the king's residence was either in South Jutland or on the island of Zealand. Very likely the author's geography was hazy on this point.

grown there in summer; "and now we shall turn back." And so they did. The earl remained at home that year. To the king it seemed strange that the earl did not come.

The following winter the king sent messengers on the same errand, and the earl promised to come. With his company he traveled to the Lim Firth. Now there were many dogs aboard the earl's ship. Then they heard the whelps barking inside the bitches.[14] The earl pronounced this to be a great portent and said that they should return, and so they did. And so that winter passed.

The third winter the king again sent men to invite the earl to his Yule feast, and he promised to come. And then the earl journeyed till he came to the Lim Firth. Then they saw a great wave rise inside the firth, and another outside. And each wave advanced against the other, and the sea grew very tumultuous, and when the waves met they clashed heavily, and the sea became all red with blood.

Then the earl said: "This is a great portent, and we shall return." And the earl remained at home during that Yuletide.

Now King Gorm waxed mightily wroth at the earl since he had not accepted his invitation, and he planned

[14] A possible reminiscence of the story of Esau and Jacob struggling in Rebekah's womb (Genesis 25:22): "and the older shall serve the younger." It is also, of course, a motif often found in folklore.

to lay waste the earl's land and thus repay him for his insult. But when Queen Thýra became aware of his plans she said it was not fitting for him to wreak vengeance on the earl and that she would give him better counsel. The king then did as the queen wished him to, sending messengers to the earl to find out the reason for his not coming. And the earl set out immediately. The king received his father-in-law in proper fashion, and both went forthwith to the council room; the king then asked him the reason for his not once coming, "and why so dishonor me and my invitation?"

The earl replied that he had not meant to insult him and that there were other reasons. And then he told the king what marvels they had seen, "and I shall now set forth to you what I think these strange happenings may portend." The king was agreeable, and the earl said: "I shall begin with our seeing in midwinter a tree with green apples hanging on it, and old and large ones lying on the ground beside it. That, I think, betokens a change of faith which will come to this land, and this faith will be fairer than the old faith, being foreshown by the fine apples. But the former faith will be laid low, like the old apples lying on the ground, and decay.

"Another marvel was the barking of whelps inside the bitches. That is likely to betoken that youths will lord it over their elders and thus grow rash and reckless; and it is likely that they will have more to say about affairs even though their elders be wiser. But I think that these youths are still unborn since the whelps were not yet dropped.

"Then there was this: that we saw great waves rise against one another with much tumult and with blood. That will betoken the discord of some men of great account within our land; and great battles will grow out of it and much turmoil, and it is more than likely that some of the strife will take place in this firth."

And the king understood the words of the earl well and they seemed wise to him, and he pardoned him, though he had readied his men to fall on the earl if his actions should be found due only to negligence. Thereupon they ended their conference. The earl remained there such time as the king wished and then journeyed home.

A little while thereafter Earl Harold gave all his dominion to his foster son Knút, and he himself journeyed south and was baptized there and never returned to his land.

4. KNÚT GORMSSON IS SLAIN IN ENGLAND

KING GORM and his son Harold fell out as soon as Harold was grown to manhood. Harold was given some ships, and he went on viking expeditions every summer but remained in Denmark during the winter.

At that time King Æthelstan ruled in England.[15] He was a good king, and old. Toward the end of his days an army of Danes invaded England, and it was headed by the sons of King Gorm, Knút and Harold. They raided the countryside in Northumberland and subdued a great realm to their rule; and they claimed it as their inheritance, because the sons of Lodbrók[16] and other forebears of theirs had possessed it.

King Æthelstan collected a great host and marched against the brothers and met them north of Cleveland and killed great numbers of Danes. But some time later the sons of Gorm went ashore at Scarborough and fought

[15] Æthelstan of England ruled from 925 to 940.

[16] According to the (unhistoric) *Ragnars saga lodbrókar*, which may be read in *The Saga of the Volsungs*, etc., tr. Margaret Schlauch (New York, 1930).

a battle there, and the Danes were victorious. Then they intended to march south to York; all the people submitted to their rule and the Danes feared no danger.

One day when the sun shone hot, men of the Danish fleet took to swimming between the ships, and likewise the two king's sons. Then there came men running down to the shore and shooting at them. Knút was struck by an arrow and wounded mortally, and they carried his body to the ship. When the country people learned of that, a huge army of them gathered. They were joined by the king, and all those who had sworn allegiance to Knút turned to King Æthelstan; and thereafter the Danes were not able to make any landing because of the host of country people gathered against them. And after that the Danes sailed back to Denmark.

At that time King Gorm was in Jutland. Harold went there immediately and told his mother the tidings. King Gorm had sworn an oath that he would die if he learned of the death of his son Knút, and that he who told the tidings would lose his life too. Then the queen had the hall draped with gray homespun. When the king came to table all those present were silent. Then the king said: "Why are all the men silent? Has anything befallen?"

Then the queen said: "Sire, you had two falcons, one white and the other gray. The white one flew far away into the wilderness, and there many crows attacked him and plucked him of all his feathers. And now the white one is gone and the gray one has returned, and it is he who will strike down birds to provide for your table."

Then King Gorm said.

> "Thus Denmark droops
> as dead is my son Knút."

Then said the queen:

> "True are the tidings
> you tell, my lord."

And all the men in the hall confirmed it. That very same hour the king fell ill, and he died at the same hour on the next day.[17] He had then been king for a hundred years. A great burial mound was thrown up over his grave. Then Harold succeeded to the rule over all his father's realm. Afterwards he drank the arvel[18] for his father and dwelt in peace for a while.

[17] Saxo Grammaticus (*ca.* 1150–1206) has a similar story in his *Gesta Danorum* about the death of Gorm the Old. However, since the inscription on the smaller Runestone of Jellinge informs us that this monument was set by Gorm in memory of his queen, he must have survived her. The alliterative scheme in the original text of the saga suggests that some old and vaguely remembered lay must have treated of this legendary motif (which is also known elsewhere). The *Gesta Danorum* can be read in Oliver Elton's translation, *The First Nine Books of the Danish History of Saxo Grammaticus* (London, 1894).

[18] The funeral feast, at which the inheritor seated himself in the High-Seat vacated by his predecessor and thus advanced into the formal (as well as *de facto*) possession of his inheritance.

5. KING HAROLD AND EARL HÁKON
PLOT TOGETHER

AT THIS TIME Harold Grayfur and his mother, Grunn-hild, ruled over Norway. And Earl Hákon Sigurdarson had fled that country with ten ships; he set out on raiding expeditions, and in the fall he came to Denmark and expressed a wish to be on friendly terms with King Harold, and the king was agreeable to that. Hákon stayed at the court of the king that winter with a hundred men.

Now Knút, the son of Gorm, was survived by a son named Harold. He was called Gold-Harold. He returned from a raiding expedition a little after Hákon's arrival, and he also had ten ships and an immense quantity of booty. He also resorted to King Harold's court. That winter, King Harold Gormsson and Earl Hákon plotted against Harold, king of Norway, and his mother, Gunnhild, and in the spring they treacherously fell upon him and overcame him in the Lim Firth, as we are told in the Book of Kings, which relates that Gold-Harold slew Harold, king of Norway.[19] Earl Hákon later on had Gold-Harold led to the gallows. Thereupon the earl assumed the rule of all Norway and was to pay tribute to the king of Denmark.

A little later, Emperor Otto of Saxland marched against Denmark with a great army, and Ólaf Tryggvason came to his aid.[20] They forced King Harold to accept Christianity, and also Earl Hákon. At that time all of Denmark was Christianized. But Earl Hákon reverted to heathendom when he had returned to Norway and never thereafter paid any tribute.

[19] It is not certain which work in the historical literature of the Old North is meant. Considering the evident marks of condensation in this passage, it appears that the author (or scribe) is satisfied merely to "refer" to the book's treatment of these events.

[20] See Introduction, page 19.

6. KING HAROLD HAS ÁKI TÓKASON SLAIN

THERE LIVED IN THE DISTRICT of Funen[21] in Denmark a
man who was called Tóki.[22] Thorvor was the name of
his wife. He had three sons. The second was called Áki,
the youngest, Palnir. The oldest, Fiolnir, was bastard-
born. Tóki was old at that time and fell ill and died, and
Thorvor, his wife, died soon thereafter. Thereupon the
two brothers Áki and Palnir took possession of their inheritance. Then Fiolnir asked his brothers what portion
of the inheritance they would let him have. They said
they would share with him the third part of the chattels
but none of the lands, and they considered that they
were giving him a fair deal. But he claimed a third of all
the property as though he were entitled to inherit. His
brothers refused. Fiolnir took that in ill part and left and

21 The large Danish island west of Zealand.
22 The name signifies "fool," just as the Swiss Tell does. Both legendary heroes were famous for their reckless bravery and prowess in
archery.

joined King Harold and became his retainer and counselor. He was a clever man and shrewd, and also malicious, and he set out to malign his brother Áki to the king.

In those days there was in Denmark no greater man not of royal birth than Áki, the son of Tóki. Every summer he went on viking expeditions, and nearly always was victorious. Fiolnir hinted to King Harold that he could not consider himself sole king of Denmark the while Áki Tókason lived. And he got the king to believe that, so there grew hostility between the king and Áki.

There was great friendship between Áki and Earl Óttar of Gotland,[23] and Áki was always welcome in Gotland. And one day he journeyed there for a banquet with two ships and a hundred followers, all well equipped with weapons and apparel. He stayed there some time, and at his departure to return to his lands he received noble gifts from the earl.

King Harold learned that Áki had gone abroad. He set forth ten ships with five hundred men and ordered them to sail and ambush Áki as he returned, and kill him and all his followers. The king's men set out and were on the lookout for Áki. To find him was an easy matter since he suspected no harm. The king's men then fell upon them all unawares, attacking them and dropping

[23] The province of southern Sweden.

the tents over their heads.²⁴ Áki and his followers were surprised and killed to a man. Afterwards the king's men brought Harold all the booty they had taken, and he was well pleased and said that now he was sole king so far as Áki was concerned. Fiolnir was glad, feeling that he was well avenged for not getting his share of the inheritance.

7. PALNIR'S MARRIAGE.
THE RISE OF PALNATÓKI

Now WHEN THESE TIDINGS were brought to Funen, Palnir was so shaken that he took to his bed, for he saw no chance of revenge against the man he had to deal with, that is, the king himself.²⁵ A man named Sigurd was a foster brother of Áki and Palnir, a wise man and wealthy. Palnir sought him out for advice, and Sigurd said he would ask a woman in marriage for him. Palnir

²⁴ Tent coverings were spread over ships when in harbor.
²⁵ There are several cases in saga literature where men of valor took to their beds when despairing of the possibility of revenge.

asked whom he had in mind. Sigurd said it was Ingeborg, the daughter of Earl Óttar of Gotland.

Palnir said: "I fear that I may not win this woman. Yet I hold that this would be the most likely redress for my misfortunes, if I could marry her."

Thereupon Sigurd set out. He had with him one ship and sixty men, and he journeyed north to Gotland. He made his errand known to the earl and asked his daughter in marriage for Palnir, saying that Palnir had abundant possessions in Funen and that he was on the verge of death because of the grief he suffered. And in the end the earl was willing to promise the hand of his daughter and said that he himself would bring her to Palnir in Funen. Then Sigurd returned and told Palnir what had passed between them, and hearing that Palnir was greatly relieved. Thereupon they prepared a great feast in Funen, not sparing in any matter. And on the day agreed, the earl arrived with a great following and the marriage was celebrated with much magnificence. Thereupon Palnir and Ingeborg were led to their marriage couch.

Ingeborg soon fell asleep and had a notable dream; and when she awoke she told Palnir her dream. "I dreamed," she said, "that I was here in this estate and that I had set up a web on the loom. It was gray of color. The weights were fixed, so it seemed, and I was weaving. Then one of the stones fell down from the middle of the web, and I saw then that the weights all were men's heads.[26] And I took up that head and recognized it."

Palnir asked whose head it was, and she said it was that of King Harold Gormsson. Palnir said it was well that she had had that dream. "I think so, likewise," she said.

When the banquet ended Earl Óttar returned to Gotland with noble gifts. A strong affection arose between Palnir and Ingeborg, and soon she bore him a son, who was called Palnatóki. He grew up in Funen and soon became wise and had many friends. And when Palnatóki was well-nigh full grown his father took ill and died. Thereupon Palnatóki assumed possession of all his father's wealth under the guardianship of his mother. Then he engaged in raiding expeditions every summer and acquired fame. And he resembled no one so much as his father's brother Áki.

At that time an earl ruled in Wales whose name was Stefnir. He had a daughter called Álof. She was wise and much beloved. Palnatóki landed there with his fleet and intended to harry in Stefnir's land. But when they learned

[26] The motif of men's heads as the weights of a loom seems a reminiscence of the famous "Song of the Valkyries" in *Njál's Saga*. (A translation of the saga, by C. F. Bayerschmidt and L. M. Hollander, was published in 1955 by New York University Press for the American-Scandinavian Foundation.)

of that, Álof and her counselor, Bjorn the Welshman, contrived the plan of asking Palnatóki to come to a banquet in his honor so that he should consider this a land of friends and not harry there. Palnatóki accepted the invitation and came to the feast with all his company. And at that feast Palnatóki asked for the hand of Álof, nor was it hard to win. And straightway they prepared for their marriage, and at the wedding Earl Stefnir bestowed on Palnatóki the title of earl and half his land; and after the earl's death Palnatóki was to have the whole of the land. Palnatóki stayed there both that summer and the winter following.[27]

In the spring he conferred with Bjorn the Welshman and said: "Now I intend to return home to Denmark, but I shall wish you to remain here with Stefnir, my father-in-law, and rule here in my stead." Then Palnatóki left together with Álof, his wife, and returned home to Funen in Denmark. There he remained settled on his estates for a while and was considered the most important man in Denmark next to the king, as well as the richest and best endowed with understanding.

[27] Historically there were Norse settlements in Wales.

8. OF KING HAROLD AND SAUMÆSA

NOW KING HAROLD went on his royal progress round about the country. Palnatóki prepared a banquet and invited him to attend it, and the king accepted and stayed there for a long time, feasting. A woman was assigned to wait on him, called Æsa and nicknamed Saumæsa.[28] She was a poor woman, yet accomplished. Then the king left the banquet and was presented with many gifts.

The following summer Saumæsa was with child, and Palnatóki spoke with her and asked who had got her with it. She answered that it was no other than the king.

"In that case," said Palnatóki, "I shall free you from work until your child is born."

Time passed, and Æsa gave birth to a boy child. He was given the name of Svein and nicknamed Saumæsu-

[28] That is, Sempstress Æsa. The following story of Svein's illegitimate origin is much like the one told by Snorri in *Heimskringla: Inga saga*, chap. 18, about the origin of the later King Hákon Sigurdarson (ruled 1157–1161), who is said to have been engendered by King Sigurd with the servant girl of a wealthy man past whose farm he was riding. The master later protected the girl and fostered her child.

Svein. He grew up on Funen, and Palnatóki and his followers were good to him. And when Svein was three years old King Harold again came to Funen for a banquet. Now Palnatóki contrived a plan with Saumæsa. One day, when the king sat at table drinking, Saumæsa approached him, leading the boy with her, and said:

"Sir King," she said, "here I bring you a boy, and I maintain that no one else is responsible for that boy but you, Sir King."

When she ceased speaking the king asked her who she was. She told him her name.

The king said: "An exceedingly bold woman you are, and a foolish one, too. And dare not say this again if you want to keep a whole skin."

Palnatóki said: "She is saying this because she considers it the truth. She is not a loose woman, and we have been protecting her for your sake."

The king answered: "I did not expect that you would side against me." "Neither do I," said Palnatóki, "and I shall keep him as though he were your son."

The king said: "I shall in nowise thank you for that." Palnatóki said: "That will make no difference. Let us now drop the matter for the present."

Then the king left the banquet, nor were any gifts made to him at parting, and there was little love lost between him and Palnatóki.

9. SVEIN'S DEALINGS WITH KING HAROLD

A SHORT TIME AFTERWARDS Álof gave birth to a son. He was named Áki and grew up with his father on Funen. Svein was there, too, until he was fifteen. Then Palnatóki bade Svein see his father and demand assistance from him and declare himself his son, whether King Harold liked it or no. Svein did as his foster father advised.

King Harold said: "I can see from your speech that they tell the truth about your mother. You are likely to be a fool and a simpleton."

Then Svein replied: "I should have preferred a mother of nobler birth if you had provided me with such a one. But you are surely my father. Now let me have three ships. My foster father will furnish me three others. If you don't do it I shall play you some evil tricks that will cost you more than the ships."

The king said: "I have a notion that I can buy you off with this so that you will never come here again."

Then the king gave him three ships with a hundred men, and Palnatóki provided him with another three ships. He harried in the realm of his father that summer, and there arose much grumbling among the farmers. The king paid no heed to it. Things went on that way till fall. Then Svein returned home to Funen and passed the winter with Palnatóki.

In the spring following, Svein again went to see King Harold; and everything went as before. Now Svein got six ships from the king, and Palnatóki gave him another six. And again Svein harried in the kingdom of his father, carrying on even more wildly than before and giving the farmers no respite. He harried both in Zealand and in Halland,[29] killing many people. These tidings spread far and wide. The farmers went to see the king about their hardships. But the king let it pass unheeded as before.

In the fall Svein repaired to Palnatóki with all his followers and remained there during the winter. When spring came he got his men ready and did exactly as his foster father advised him: he went to the king and asked for twelve ships.

The king said: "I have never seen the like of you for impudence—that you dare to come to me, being a thief

[29] The province of Sweden opposite northern Jutland. It formerly belonged to Denmark.

and a robber. And never will I acknowledge you as my kinsman."

Svein said: "Most certainly am I your son, and in truth we are kinsmen. But I shall not spare you for all that. Right now I shall fight you if you don't give me what I want, nor will it help you to back out now."

"You are a difficult man to deal with," the king said, "and your ways show that you are of no mean birth. You shall have what you demand. Take yourself off, then, and never again come within my sight."

Then Svein betook himself to Palnatóki with thirty ships, and was made right welcome. Palnatóki said: "It appears that you turn my advice to good account. Now you are to make forays on Denmark this summer, and all the more since now you have greater forces. The king is not likely to bear with you longer; but do not flee even though he pursue you with an army, because I shall come to your aid. I intend to sail to Wales this summer, with nine ships, to stay with my father-in-law, Earl Stefnir."

Thereupon they parted, leaving the country at the same time. Now Svein laid waste Denmark, both day and night, robbing and killing people and burning the countryside. The inhabitants fled from this sad havoc and informed the king, and he was not willing to stand for it any longer. He had fifty ships made ready and went with the fleet himself, and they made search for Svein.

In the fall the two fleets met at the island of Born-holm.[30] It was so late in the evening that neither could see to do battle. But in the morning, as soon as there was enough light, they laid their ships broadside and fought all day till evening. By that time ten ships of King Harold's were cleared of their crew, and twelve of Svein's. Then Svein retired with his ships to the inner end of the bight, and the king anchored his ships across the bay and shut Svein in.

10. PALNATÓKI SLAYS KING HAROLD AND PROCLAIMS SVEIN KING

THAT SAME EVENING Palnatóki made a landfall there with twenty-four ships. He anchored on the other side of the island, nearby the headland, and pitched his tents there. Then Palnatóki went up on land by himself. He had with him his bow and his quiver. That same evening

[30] The shoreline of the island of Bornholm (in the Baltic, south of Sweden) shows no indentation capable of harboring a fleet, nor a promontory such as is mentioned in the following narrative. Actually, the battle between father and son took place at Helgenæs Headland on the east coast of central Jutland.

King Harold went up on land, accompanied by eleven others, and into the forest and kindled a fire to bask at. It was dark night by then. The king took off his clothes and warmed himself at the fire. Palnatóki saw the fire in the forest and circled near it. He recognized the men and fixed an arrow in his bow and shot King Harold through. The king dropped dead straightway. Palnatóki at once returned to his men.

The followers of the king thronged about his body and took counsel how they should proceed.

Fiolnir said: "It is my advice that we all tell the same story: that the king was shot in battle; for then we shall not be reproached for our negligence." And this they all bound themselves to do. Fiolnir took the arrow to keep it—it was easily known from other arrows because it was wound with gold.

Meanwhile, Palnatóki told off twenty of his men to come with him, saying that he was going to look for Svein. They went across the cape, and he and Svein took counsel together. Svein said that he would follow Palnatóki's advice.

Palnatóki told no one about the death of the king. He said: "It will not take us long to decide on a plan. I shall join you on your ship. Then we shall undo all your ships from their fastenings[31] and make an attack on the king's fleet. I dislike being penned in here by the king and killed." They followed that plan and rowed to the attack. Three swift-sailing ships in the king's fleet foundered, and of their crews only those who could swim escaped with their lives. Palnatóki and Svein rowed through that gap with all Svein's ships and joined the fleet that Palnatóki had brought with him.

Next morning they attacked the king's fleet and learned that the king was dead. Then said Palnatóki: "Now you can choose one of two things, either to fight us or to accept Svein as king."

They chose to accept Svein. Then both fleets sailed, and an assembly was called, and there Svein was chosen king over all Denmark.

[31] Ships were fastened together for battle with hawsers.

11. PALNATÓKI ACKNOWLEDGES HIS ARROW

Now WHEN SVEIN had become king it appeared fitting to him to honor his father with a funeral feast, and he invited Palnatóki to come to it. But Palnatóki said that he could not come before the beginning of winter, "because news has reached me that Stefnir, my father-in-law, is dead, and all his realm falls to me."

So the arvel came to nought that fall. Palnatóki departed, leaving his son Áki to govern his land in Funen. He commended Áki to King Svein's particular care. The king gave him his promise and kept his word. Then Palnatóki sailed to Wales and took over the rule of it; and thus the year passed.

The summer after, King Svein sent messengers to Palnatóki to invite him to the arvel. But Palnatóki said he was still unable to come; so the funeral feast came to nought that year too. The following summer King Svein again made preparations for the funeral feast, and again sent men to Palnatóki to bid him, and to say that he would resent it if he did not come.

Palnatóki told the messengers that now he would come and that the king should make ready for the feast. Then the king prepared for it and invited a host of people. And when all was ready, the day wore on, and still Palnatóki did not come. So men sat down to drink. The king assigned a place for Palnatóki on the high-seat opposite himself, and seats for his followers from there to the door. And then the king and his men began to drink.

Now to tell about Palnatóki and Bjorn the Welshman: with three ships and a hundred men, half of them Danes and half Welshmen, they made land that evening. The weather was fine. They turned the prows of their ships seaward, fastening them with cables from the stern, and laid the oars into the rowlocks. Then they all went up to the king's hall. Palnatóki with all his followers entered and greeted the king. The king welcomed Palnatóki cordially and bade him and his men take the seats he had assigned them. And then the banquet began.

Fiolnir leaned over to the king and spoke to him a while under his breath. The king changed color, his face turning as red as blood.

A man called Arnodd, one of the king's attendants, was standing near the table. Fiolnir handed him an arrow and bade him carry it to all the men in the hall until some one would acknowledge it. Arnodd went first to the center of the hall where the king sat, then toward the door. Then he returned toward the center and stood before Palnatóki and asked him whether he perchance recognized this arrow.

Palnatóki said: "Why should I not know my own arrow? Let me have it, it is mine."

Deep silence reigned in the hall, to hear some one acknowledge this arrow as his own.

The king said: "You, Palnatóki, where did you part with this arrow, the last time you shot it?"

Palnatóki replied: "Often have I been indulgent to you, foster son, and so it shall be this time: I parted with it from my bowstring the time I shot your father through with it."

The king said: "Stand up, my men, at once, and lay hands on Palnatóki and his followers. They shall be killed, all of them. There is now an end to the good relations between us."

Thereupon all the men in the hall leaped to their feet.

Palnatóki then drew his sword and cut his kinsman Fiolnir in two. He and his men gained the door, because every man there was so much his friend that no one wanted to harm him. So Palnatóki and all his followers managed to get out of the hall, except one man of Bjorn's company.

Palnatóki said: "That is the best we could have expected. Now let us hurry down to our ships."

Bjorn said: "You would not thus leave your own man in the lurch, nor will I."

He went back into the hall. There the king's men were tossing the Welshman into the air and had well-nigh torn him to pieces. Then Bjorn got hold of the dead man and put him on his back and returned with him to his men. He did that mostly for glory's sake.

12. THE FOUNDING OF JÓMSBORG

THEN THEY ALL RETURNED to their ships and fell to rowing, and got away; nor did they stop till they were back home in Wales. But King Svein and his men continued with the funeral feast, and he was galled with the turn events had taken.

The summer after, Álof, Palnatóki's wife, fell ill and died. And then Palnatóki was content no longer to stay in Wales, and he set Bjorn the Welshman to rule the land for him. He himself left with thirty ships and took to harrying in Scotland and Ireland. And this course he pursued for three years, acquiring great wealth and fame. The fourth summer, Palnatóki sailed east to Wendland[32] with forty ships.

A king ruled there at that time whose name was Burisleif.[33] He learned of Palnatóki's approach and was ill pleased to have him harry there because Palnatóki was well-nigh always victorious and had more fame than any other man. So the king sent messengers inviting him to the court and offering him friendship. And to his invitation he added the offer of a district in his land called Jóm,[34] if Palnatóki would rule and settle there and defend the king's land.

Palnatóki accepted this offer and settled there with all his men. And soon he had a great and strong fortification made. A part of it jutted out to sea, and in that part there was a harbor, big enough to accommodate three hundred warships, so that the ships could be locked within the fortification. With great skill a portal was designed with a stone arch above it and before it an iron portcullis which could be locked from inside the harbor. And on top of the stone arch there was a great strong-

[32] That is, the littoral of the southern Baltic, present-day Mecklenburg and Pomerania, formerly inhabited by Slavic tribes.

[33] The Old Norse form for Boleslav (the First, 992–1025).

[34] On the island of Wollin in the estuary of the Oder River, though the precise location is not known. The fortress was somewhere near the town of Julin, an important center in those days of commerce between the north and the south, which had been founded to exact toll from all shipments in transit.

hold, and within the stronghold were catapults. The whole fort was called Jómsborg.

Then Palnatóki established laws for Jómsborg, with the assistance of wise men, to the end that the renown of the men of Jómsborg should spread most widely and their power should wax greatly. The first of their laws was that no one might join the company who was over fifty or under eighteen. All members were to be between these ages. Kinship must not weigh when considering for membership a man who wished to join. No member was to flee from any man who was his equal in bravery and as well armed as himself. Each member must avenge any other member as though he were his brother. No one was to utter words of fear or be afraid of anything, however hopeless matters looked. All the booty brought in from their expeditions was to be carried to the standard—of whatever value, big or small—and anyone not abiding by this rule must leave the company. No one within the fort was to start a quarrel. And if news of importance came to any man's knowledge he was not to have the temerity to make it known to all, because Palnatóki was to announce all news. No one was to have a woman within the fort, and no one was to be away for more than three days. And if it became known after a man had been admitted into the company that he had earlier slain the father or brother or some other near kinsman of a member, Palnatóki was to be the judge, as he was to be also of whatever other differences arose among them.

In this wise they had their quarters in the fort and kept their laws well. Every summer they went on viking expeditions to various countries and won renown. They were considered the greatest of warriors, with hardly any their equals in that time, and were called the Jómsvíkings.

13. OF EARL STRÚT-HAROLD AND VÉSETI AND THEIR SONS

AT THAT TIME there ruled in the island of Zealand an earl by the name of Harold. He was nicknamed Strút-Harold,[35] because he owned a hat which was adorned with gold ornaments ten marks in weight.[36] Ingeborg was the name of his wife, and their sons were Sigvaldi and Thorkel the Tall. Their daughter was called Tova.

A man called Véseti ruled over the island of Bornholm. His wife was named Hildigunn, and their sons

[35] Old Norse *strútr* signifies the pointed crest of a helmet.
[36] One mark was equivalent to eight ounces.

were Búi and Sigurd Cape. They had a daughter called Thorgunn.

Áki, the son of Palnatóki, lived on the island of Funen. King Svein, who was kind to Áki in every respect, asked Thorgunn in marriage for him. The marriage of Áki and Thorgunn was a very happy one, and they had a son named Vagn.[37]

Now Vagn was only a few years old when it became known that he was more difficult to handle than any other youth. He beat and manhandled every one. He lived, now at home, now on Bornholm with his maternal grandfather, Véseti. Neither his parents nor his grandfather seemed able to control him. Among all his kinsmen he got along best with Búi his maternal uncle, and would do what Búi told him, but would heed no others. Vagn was exceedingly handsome and most accomplished in all manner of things. He had great strength.

Búi was a man of few words and proud of mind. Few knew exactly how strong he was. He was not handsome, but he was personable. Sigurd Cape, his brother, was a handsome man, of great courage, and very taciturn.

Sigvaldi, the son of Earl Harold, was sallow-faced. He had very fine eyes but an ugly nose.[38] He was a man of

[37] Probably from the Welsh *vaughn*, "little." Note the Welsh family connection.

[38] Reference in a pert squib to Sigvaldi's long, crooked nose and to

great height, and brisk in his motions. His brother Thorkel likewise was exceedingly tall and strong, and both brothers were very shrewd.

Sigvaldi and Thorkel asked their father whether he thought it advisable for them to join the company at Jómsborg. The earl said yes, "and it is high time for you to make trial of yourselves." They asked him if he would outfit them with weapons and provisions. The earl replied that they should provide for themselves or not go at all. They wanted to go none the less. They made ready two ships with a hundred men and chose and equipped them as best they could. Then they sailed to Bornholm. There they made a landing and plundered the best farm Véseti owned, robbing it of all movable property and carrying the booty to their ships. No more is told of their doings till they arrived at Jómsborg.

It was the custom of Palnatóki to go with a great company to the battlement that had been built over the channel into the harbor and from there talk to whoever approached the fort. When he learned of the coming of Sigvaldi and his men, Palnatóki entered the battlement with a great host and asked who was in command of the ships.

Sigvaldi said: "They are captained by two brothers,

his record of treachery cost the Icelandic skald Stefnir Thorgilsson his life.

the sons of Earl Strút-Harold. And our business here is that we want to join your company, with whatever men among us you may be able to use."

Palnatóki took counsel with the men in his company. He said he knew the visitors' kinsfolk and that they were of high birth. The company asked Palnatóki to decide. Thereupon the gates were opened and the ships were rowed into the fort. Then the men were tested. One half of the crew was found to be usable. The other half departed. Thereupon the brothers and their followers were inducted into the laws of the company.

Now we shall go back to where Véseti was plundered of his farm. He journeyed to King Svein and told him what had happened, enjoining his sons from doing any violence meanwhile. The king advised him to do nothing just now; "but I shall send word to Earl Strút-Harold and find out whether he will make good the damage his sons have done, so as to make amends to you; and in that case I would have you be satisfied with that."

Thereupon Véseti sailed home. King Svein sent messengers to Earl Harold to bid him come to court. And the king told the earl what his sons had done to Véseti and bade him make good Véseti's loss, and said that afterwards the peace must be kept.

The earl said: "As yet I have not received the goods for which I am supposed to repay; and it is none of my business if young men carry off some cattle or sheep to provision themselves."

The king said: "In that case you may journey home. I have told you what my wish is. You must now rely on yourself to defend yourself and your property against Véseti and his sons."

Earl Harold said that he was not afraid of Véseti and his sons. Then he journeyed home.

Véseti and his sons learned about the conference of Harold with the king. They made ready three ships as best they could, with a crew of two hundred men. Then they sailed to Zealand and there ransacked three of the finest farms owned by Earl Harold and then returned home. Now Earl Harold learned that his farms had been raided. He sent messengers to King Svein, saying that he would now gladly have him make peace for him with Véseti.

King Svein said: "Let Earl Harold follow his own good counsel since he spurned mine. I will have nothing more to do with the matter now."

The messengers returned and told Harold how matters stood. The earl said: "In that case we shall have to take our own counsel, if the king sits idly by."

Thereupon Earl Harold equipped ten ships and sailed to Bornholm and looted three farms of Véseti's which were in no wise poorer than the ones Véseti had raided.

Then he returned and considered that things had gone well, beyond expectation.

14. KING SVEIN ARBITRATES THE FEUD

VÉSETI LEARNED about these happenings and at once went to the king. The king welcomed him warmly.

Then Véseti said: "Matters have now come to such a pass between Earl Harold and me that I fear there will be war between our countrymen if you do not lend a hand in the matter. Maybe you would find that more advisable now than later."

The king said: "I shall very shortly journey to the Íseyrar Assembly,[39] and I shall summon to it Earl Harold, and then you two are to make up."

Thereupon Véseti returned home. Time passed, and then the assembly was held. King Svein came to it with a great host of men, because he meant to be sole judge between the two parties. He had fifty ships. Earl Harold had but a short way to come, and he brought twenty ships. Véseti also came to the assembly. He had only five ships, and his sons were not with him.

[39] On the island of Zealand.

Earl Harold had pitched his tents at some little distance from the sea, and Véseti had set his by the sea, close to the sound near the place of assembly. And as the evening wore on, ten ships were seen sailing from the direction of Earl Harold's residence. They made fast in the roadstead. Aboard the fleet were the sons of Véseti, and they and their men went up to the assembly. Búi was splendidly appareled, for he wore Earl Harold's robes of state that were worth twenty marks in gold, and on his head he had the earl's hat with ornaments worth ten marks of gold. Two chests had also been taken from the earl, and in each were ninety marks of gold. The men advanced to the assembly fully armed and in battle array.

Then Búi spoke as follows: "Now you have the chance, Earl Harold, if you have the courage to fight and the manhood, to seize your arms, for now I am ready to fight you."

King Svein heard Búi's words and realized that he could not maintain his authority if this came to pass; so he went between the two forces and they did not get to do battle. And the outcome was that both parties had to agree to the king's arbitration. But Búi insisted that, in any settlement, he would never let go of the earl's chests of gold, and everyone knew that he was the man to stick to that.

Thereupon the king made known his decision for reconciling them, and it was as follows: "that you, Búi, are to give up Earl Harold's robes of state; his two chests of gold you may keep. And the three farms of Earl Harold that you and your kinsmen raided, you are to repay in this wise: the earl is to marry his daughter Tova to Sigurd Cape, and these three farms shall be her dowry."

Both parties accepted this decision with a good grace. Véseti gave Sigurd a third of all the property which had been taken by Earl Harold's sons, and Sigurd was exceedingly well pleased with the wife he got. They straightway proceeded from the assembly to celebrate the marriage, and King Svein was invited to it by both parties. Then the marriage of Sigurd and Tova was celebrated with much splendor.

15. BÚI, SIGVALDI, AND VAGN JOIN THE JÓMSVÍKINGS

THEN VÉSETI SAILED HOME and dwelt there in peace. But when Búi and Sigurd had been at home a short time Búi grew eager to go to Jómsborg and so achieve more fame. Sigurd also wanted to go, though he was married. Then the two brothers made ready to leave. They had two ships and a hundred and twenty men. It was their plan to proceed as the sons of Strút-Harold had done. They arrived at Jómsborg and made fast outside the portals of the harbor. The chieftains of the company went up into the battlement with a great host. Sigvaldi recognized the newcomers. Then Búi announced his purpose, saying that he would like to join the company, if Palnatóki would accept him and his brother.

Then Sigvaldi said: "How did you and Strút-Harold settle affairs before you kinsmen left Denmark?"

Búi replied: "It would take a long time to tell about our dealings, and so I shall not relate them; but we are reconciled now according to the king's arbitration."

Then Palnatóki said to his men: "Would you chance it that these men are speaking the truth? I am eager to have them, because few are likely to be their equals in our company."

They replied: "We are agreed that you allow them into fellowship with us. If any matter should come up later about their affairs of which we know nothing, then we shall leave that, as other matters, to your decision."

Thereupon the stronghold was opened for them, and Búi and his brother made fast their ships in the harbor. Afterwards their company was tried, and eighty of their men were considered up to the mark, but forty went back home. Then all the company resided in the stronghold with great renown, and went forth on viking expeditions every summer and achieved many a deed of valor.

Now it is told of Vagn Ákason that he stayed alternately with his father and with Véseti, his maternal grandfather. He was of such an ungovernable disposition that by the time he was nine years he had killed three men. He stayed at home till he was twelve. Then he asked his father to let him have a company of men, and Áki gave him sixty men and a ship, and Véseti, too, gave him sixty men and another warship. No one of those in his company was older than twenty, and no one younger than eighteen except Vagn himself, who was twelve. He declared he would himself look out for provisions and weapons for them.

Thereupon he sailed forth to procure weapons and food. He sailed along the whole length of Denmark, raiding the countryside ruthlessly, robbing arms and war gear, and did not stop before he had enough of both. Then he set his course for Jómsborg and arrived there early in the day at sunrise. He moored his ships by the stone arch, and the chieftains of the stronghold came out with a great following and asked who were the men who had come there. In reply, Vagn asked whether Palnatóki was in the fort. Palnatóki answered that he was, "and who are you who behave in such grand fashion?"

Vagn said: "I shall not conceal from you that my name is Vagn and that I am the son of Áki; I have come here to offer you my company of men, and I was not considered easy to deal with at home."

Palnatóki said: "Does it seem likely to you, kinsman, that you can get along with men here, seeing that your own folk at home could scarcely deal with you?"

Vagn said: "They have told me wrong about you, kinsman, if such men as these would be of no use in your company."

Then Palnatóki said to his men: "Would you consider it wise for us to take them into our company?"

"It would seem advisable to me," said Búi, "even though he got along best with me of all his kinsmen, that we do not take him in."

Palnatóki said: "Kinsman Vagn, our men are set against you, your kinsmen as well as the others."

Vagn said: "I did not expect that of you, kinsman Búi."

Búi said: "I shall stand on it, though."

Vagn said: "And what do the sons of Strút-Harold say about it?"

Sigvaldi said: "We are agreed, both of us, that you shall never get into our band."

Then Palnatóki asked: "How old are you, kinsman?"

Vagn replied: "I shall not lie about it; I am twelve."

Palnatóki said: "That shows that you do not mean to abide by our laws: you are much younger than any one we have accepted into our company. And so that settles the matter; you cannot stay here."

Vagn said: "I don't want to insist on your going against your laws. But they would hardly be broken, since I am as good as a man eighteen years old or older."

Palnatóki said: "Don't insist, kinsman. I shall, rather, send you to Wales to Bjorn. And because of our kinship I shall let you have half of my possessions in Wales."

Vagn said: "A noble offer, but I won't have it."

Palnatóki said: "What, then, do you want if you don't want that?"

"That I shall let you know now," Vagn said. "I challenge Sigvaldi, the son of Strút-Harold, to come out of the fort with two ships and try conclusions with us and see who yields and who has the better of the fight. And let it be agreed between us that you shall take us into your company if his ships flee; in the contrary case I shall go away. And I stress that I challenge Sigvaldi to do battle with us unless he is an arrant coward and has the heart of a she-animal rather than that of a man."[40]

Palnatóki said: "Do you hear, Sigvaldi, what Vagn

[40] To be called a she-animal was the most deadly insult that could be offered a man.

says? He is not so gentle in his terms of challenge, either. And I am thinking you will have a tough test. But since so much has been said about the matter already I will not stand in the way of your attacking his ships and doing them all the damage you can. Only, I do not want you to kill Vagn, even though he may not be altogether easy to deal with."

Thereupon Sigvaldi and his men put on their war gear and rowed out with two ships. And at once a fierce battle began. Vagn and his crew hurled such a volley of stones that Sigvaldi and his men could do nothing but protect themselves and were hard put to it to do even that. Then they lay broadside to broadside. And when Vagn and his crew ran out of stones they fell upon their opponents with sword blows, and Sigvaldi was obliged to order his ships to fall back to land for more stones. But

Vagn and his crew were right after them and attacked them on land, so that Sigvaldi had to give ground and there was a still fiercer battle. Many of Sigvaldi's troop fell.

Meanwhile Palnatóki and his men were watching the combat from the fort. It seemed clear to Palnatóki what course matters would take, and he called on Sigvaldi to stop the fight, "for it will not do for you two to keep on with this. My advice is that we take Vagn and his men into our company even though he is younger than is permitted by our laws, and unless my judgment deceives me we may well expect that this man will become a valiant fighter."

Thereupon Sigvaldi's men did as Palnatóki said. They left off fighting, and Vagn and his men were taken into the company and its laws. Thirty of Sigvaldi's men had fallen, but few of Vagn's, though many were wounded. After that Vagn, in command of a ship, went with the company on every expedition, and no one seemed to be his equal as a fighter.

16. OF PALNATÓKI'S DEATH AND SIGVALDI'S AMBITION

THIS CONTINUED for three years, until Vagn was fifteen years old. Then Palnatóki took sick. He sent messengers to King Burisleif to come to him. And when the king arrived Palnatóki said: "I am thinking, Sir King, that this will be my last sickness."

The king said: "In that case it is my advice that you choose some one in your stead to look after matters as you have done and that he be chieftain in the fort and that the company stay here as before." Palnatóki said that all in all Sigvaldi was the man best fitted to take command, "yet it seems to me that all of them fall somewhat short of what I have been."

The king said: "Often your counsels have benefited us, and now I shall follow your last one. Let all laws stand as before in the fort."

Sigvaldi was by no means loath, and in fact mightily pleased, to assume command.

Then Palnatóki gave his kinsman Vagn half of his earldom in Wales to govern under the guardianship of

Bjorn the Welshman, and commended him to the special care of the company. And shortly thereafter Palnatóki died, and that was felt by all to be a great loss.

Sigvaldi had administered the laws but a short while when breaches in the discipline began to occur. Women stayed at Jómsborg two or three nights at a time; and men remained away longer from the fort than when Palnatóki lived. Also, there were maimings once in a while, and even some killings.

King Burisleif had three daughters. The oldest was called Ástrid and she was both exceedingly beautiful and exceedingly wise. Another was called Gunnhild, and the third was Geira—she who later married King Ólaf Tryggvason. Sigvaldi came to King Burisleif and presented this proposition: he would remain no longer in the fort, unless he was given the king's daughter Ástrid in marriage.

"It had been my intention," said the king, "to marry her to some one of more princely rank than yours; yet I need you in the fort. We shall take it all under advisement."

He sought his daughter Ástrid and asked her whether it suited her wishes to be married to Sigvaldi.

Ástrid replied: "To say the truth, it would never be my choice to marry Sigvaldi. Therefore if he is to win my hand he must relieve us of all the tribute this land has been paying the Danish king before he may enter the marriage bed with me. There is a second condition too: he must lure King Svein here so that you will have him in your power."

Then Burisleif made this clear to Sigvaldi, who was nevertheless bent on marrying Ástrid. The upshot was that he accepted the conditions, and they made a binding agreement about it. He was to fulfill the conditions before the first days of Yule or the agreement would be null and void.

17. SIGVALDI CAPTURES KING SVEIN

THEREUPON SIGVALDI returned to Jómsborg. And a short while thereafter he set sail from the fort with three ships and three hundred men and continued till he came to Zealand. He learned from people there that King Svein was being given a banquet, not far away. Sigvaldi moored his ships by a tongue of land. No other ships lay near the estate where the king sat banqueting, accompanied by six hundred of his men.

Sigvaldi turned his ships so that their prows pointed

away from land, and fastened them together broadside to broadside. Then he sent twenty men as messengers to King Svein—"and tell him that I am sick unto death and would at all costs see him, and that his life depends on that."

They came to the king and delivered their message. The king started out at once with all his men. When Sigvaldi learned that the king had arrived he was lying on the ship farthest from land. He said to his men: "When thirty men have boarded the ship nearest to shore you are to pull up the gangplank and say that no more must crowd on lest the ship sink—and I surmise the king will be among the foremost. And when twenty men have entered the middle ship you are to pull up the gangplank between it and the first one."

Now the king stepped aboard the ship, and Sigvaldi's men did as they were told. And when the king reached Sigvaldi's ship with only ten men he asked whether Sigvaldi was still able to speak and was told that he was very low. Thereupon the king went up to Sigvaldi's couch and asked whether he could speak.

Sigvaldi said: "Bend down to me."

When the king bent down over him Sigvaldi with one arm took hold of him about his shoulders and with the other gripped him under the arm. At the same time he called out to all the crews to cast off double-quick, and so they did. The king's men were left standing behind on land and could only look helplessly on.

Then the king said: "How now, Sigvaldi, are you going to betray me? Or have you something else in mind?"

Sigvaldi said: "I shall not betray you; but you shall come to Jómsborg with me, and there you will be welcome and we shall show you all honor."

The king said: "That I shall have to comply with."

So they sailed to Jómsborg, and the Jómsvíkings prepared a grand festival on his arrival and declared themselves to be his men.

Afterwards, Sigvaldi told King Svein that he had asked, in his behalf, for the hand of that daughter of King Burisleif whose name was Gunnhild and who was the most beautiful; "and to me he has betrothed her sister, Ástrid. Now I shall journey to him to carry through this business for you."

The king asked him to do so. Thereupon Sigvaldi set out with one hundred and twenty of his men and had a conference with King Burisleif. Sigvaldi pointed out that now he had fulfilled the conditions for marrying Ástrid. And the king and he laid their plans together, whereupon Sigvaldi returned to Jómsborg.

King Svein asked how his suit was progressing. Sigvaldi said that it depended altogether on King Svein himself: "whether you, Sir King, will remit all of King

Burisleif's tribute to you—then he will give you the hand of his daughter. Besides, it would be more fitting to your honor and his if the king whose daughter you marry does not have to pay you tribute."

And so persuasive was Sigvaldi in his representations that the king was willing to accept this condition. The day for the marriage feast was agreed on, and both weddings were to be on the same day. King Svein then proceeded to the feast, followed by all the Jómsvíkings, and it was so splendid that no one remembered a more glorious one ever celebrated in Wendland.

The first evening, both brides wore their head coverings low over their faces;[41] but the morning after, both brides were gay and had their faces uncovered. And now King Svein examined their countenances, for he had seen neither one before. Sigvaldi had said that Gunnhild was the more beautiful; but it did not seem so to the king, and he realized that Sigvaldi had not told him the truth. And now he grasped Sigvaldi's designs. However, he made the best of a bad bargain. And when the feast came to an end the king sailed home with his bride, and had with him thirty ships and a great host of men and many valuable gifts. Sigvaldi journeyed to Jómsborg with his bride, and the Jómsvíkings with him.

[41] As was the custom; cf. the Eddic "Lay of Thrym," stanza 26, in *The Poetic Edda,* tr. Hollander (The University of Texas, 1928).

18. THE VOWS OF THE JÓMSVIKINGS

A LITTLE WHILE LATER the news came from Denmark that Earl Strút-Harold, the father of Sigvaldi and Thorkel, had died. Their brother Heming was still young, so King Svein sent messengers to Sigvaldi to say that he and Thorkel should return to Denmark to inherit their father. They sent word for the king to prepare the arvel feast and not be sparing with their goods, and that they themselves would arrive at the beginning of the winter season. This plan seemed unwise to most of their men, for they suspected that the friendship between King Svein and Sigvaldi was not too solid, the way things had gone. But the brothers would not hear of not going.

The Jómsvíkings departed with sixty ships and sailed to Zealand. King Svein was there already and had prepared a splendid feast, and a huge force of men was assembled. The very first night King Svein saw to it that the Jómsvíkings were served the most powerful drink, and they took to it fast and furiously. When the king saw that they were dead drunk and very talkative he spoke as follows:

"There is good cheer here now, and it would seem fitting if we chose some pastime to entertain all those here, one which would live in men's minds in after times."

Sigvaldi said: "Then it seems to us best, to begin with, that you make the first choice, for we all owe allegiance to you."

The king said: "I know that it is customary at such celebrations for men to make vows so as to increase their renown. And since you Jómvíkings are famed in all lands it is likely that your vows will surpass all others. Now I shall make the beginning: I vow that I shall have driven King Æthelræd of England from his kingdom before the beginning of next winter or else have slain him and thus obtained his kingdom.[42] Now it is your turn, Sigvaldi. And make your vow not less."

Sigvaldi said that so it should be. "Sire, I make the vow that before three years have passed I shall have harried in Norway with such forces as I have, and have driven Earl Hákon out of his land or killed him, or else have fallen myself."

Then the king said: "Now this is as it should be. That is a brave vow—all luck to you to carry it out well. Now it is your turn, Thorkel the Tall, and you will have to make your vow a handsome one."

[42] Æthelræd's rule (978–1016) was one long warfare against the Scandinavian invaders.

Thorkel said: "I have considered it, and this it is: to accompany my brother Sigvaldi and not flee before I see the stern of his ship."

"Nobly spoken," said the king, "and you are likely to perform it well. And now it is your turn, Búi the Stout, and let your vow be one that is noteworthy."

"This vow I make," said Búi, "to support Sigvaldi in this expedition to the best of my power and to hold out as long as he does."

"It is as we thought," said the king. "Manful deeds could be expected of you. It is your turn now, Sigurd Cape, after your brother."

"That is quickly done," said Sigurd. "I shall follow my brother and not flee before he flees or has fallen."

"That was to be expected from you," said the king. "Now it is your turn, Vagn. And we are eager to hear what your vow will be, because you kinsfolk are men of great mettle."

Vagn said: "My vow is that I shall follow Sigvaldi and Búi, my kinsman, on this expedition and hold out as long as Búi does and is alive; and another thing I vow is that if I get to Norway I shall kill Thorkel Leira[43] and get into the bed of his daughter Ingeborg without the consent of her kinsfolk."

[43] Leira means "mudflat."

Bjorn the Welshman was there with Vagn. Then the king said: "What vow do you make, Bjorn?"

He replied: "To follow my foster-son Vagn with all my might."

That was the end of their talks. Then all sought their couches. Sigvaldi went to bed with his wife Ástrid, and he soon fell asleep and slept soundly. When he awoke, Ástrid asked him whether he remembered what vows he had made. He said he remembered nothing.

She said: "It will not do for you to pretend that you made none." And she told him what they were. "And we shall need to set all our wits to work."

Sigvaldi said: "What are we to do? You are both wise and resourceful."

"I don't know," she said, "but we must contrive something, for you will get few reinforcements from King Svein if you don't get them right now."

Then together they laid their plans. Soon King Svein took his seat in the banquet hall, and all the Jómvíkings joined him. Sigvaldi was in a very cheerful mood. Then the king asked Sigvaldi whether he remembered the vows he had made. Sigvaldi said he did not remember, and the king told him what they were. Sigvaldi replied that one was not responsible for what one said over the cups, "but what would you contribute to help me fulfill my vows?"

The king said that he might contribute twenty ships when Sigvaldi was all ready.

Sigvaldi said: "That is good enough from a franklin but not from a king."

Then King Svein said, and wrinkled his brows: "How many would you have?"

"That is quickly said," Sigvaldi answered. "Sixty large ships; and I shall furnish as many to match them, though smaller.[44] Because it is not certain that all will return."

Then the king said: "All the ships will be ready as soon as you are."

"Very good," said Sigvaldi, "and be sure you live up to your promise, for we shall depart at once—as soon as this banquet comes to an end."

The king grew very quiet, then said, more quickly than might have been expected: "It shall be so. Yet this has come to pass sooner than I had thought."

Then said Ástrid, Sigvaldi's wife: "There would be little hope of overcoming Earl Hákon if you did not act before he has any inkling of our plan." Then and there at the banquet they made arrangements for the expedition.

Tova, the daughter of Earl Strút-Harold, said to Sigurd, her husband: "This I shall ask of you, that you

---

[44] Assuming the average crew of a warship to have been fifty men, it will be seen that considerable forces were engaged in the later battle.

follow your brother Búi as best you can. He has shown me many kindnesses, and I shall try to make a small return for them. I have here two men whom I will give you, Búi. One is called Hávard the Hewing, the other, Áslák Holmskalli."

Búi accepted the gift of the two men and thanked her for it. He straightway gave Áslák to his kinsman Vagn.

19. GEIRMUND ESCAPES AND WARNS EARL HÁKON

NOW THE BANQUET came to an end, and the Jómsvíkings immediately prepared to leave. Then they set sail with one hundred and twenty large ships. They had a favorable breeze and soon made Víken[45] in Norway. Late in the evening they arrived at the town of Túnsberg, and took it by surprise.

Geirmund the White was the name of the magistrate who had charge of the defense of Túnsberg. When the Jómsvíkings entered the town they laid it waste almost completely. They killed many and plundered an immense

[45] The present Oslofjord.

amount of property, so that the townsmen had a sad awakening.

Geirmund awoke, and also those men who slept in the quarters nearest to his. They ran up into a loft that they thought could be defended longest. Then the Jómsvíkings rushed to the loft and chopped at it most furiously.[46] Geirmund saw that the defenders could not hold out there long, so he quickly made up his mind—he jumped down from the loft into the street, landing on his feet. Vagn happened to be standing right there and straightway slashed out with his sword and cut off Geirmund's hand, and there was a gold ring on the hand.

Geirmund escaped to the forests and traveled through them for six days. Then he came out to inhabited places and journeyed in a northerly direction as fast as he could, both day and night. He learned that Earl Hákon with a following of one hundred and twenty men was banqueting at an estate called á Skugga.[47] He arrived there late in the evening and found the earl at table drinking.

Geirmund went up to him and greeted him. The earl asked him who he was, and Geirmund told him. The earl asked if he had any news.

[46] Many of the houses were erected on stout wooden pillars, as is still the case with the Norwegian *stabbur* or provision houses.

[47] That is (freely), "Shady-Side."

Geirmund said: "Small news, as yet; but it may become big news."

The earl said: "What is it?"

Geirmund said: "An army has come to the land east in Víken, and it is spreading death and destruction."

Then the earl said: "I know that you would not tell news of war unless it was the truth. Who commands this army?"

"Sigvaldi is the name of the commander," Geirmund answered, "and I heard mentioned the names of Búi and Vagn. And I have a reminder of all this." He lifted up his arm, showing the stump.

The earl said: "A nasty trick they have played on you. Do you know who gave you this wound?"

Geirmund said: "I can make a very likely guess, because when the man who did it picked up the ring that was on the hand they said, 'There you made a haul, Vagn'—so they said. And I believe that this is the host called the Jómsvíkings."

"You are likely to be right about that," the earl said. "And it is the last thing I could wish."

The earl at once left the banquet and made for Raumsdale. He sent men in all directions with the war-arrow.[48] Also he sent messengers north to Drontheim to tell his

[48] The war-arrow was borne from farm to farm as a token of summons to war service.

· 91

son Svein to gather forces in that district. And his son
Earl Eric journeyed north to Naumudale and then north
by the sea around North Möre and the islands. The army
was to gather at the island called Hod. Erling, another
son of the earl, went about Rogaland district, and Earl
Hákon himself, around South Möre and Raumsdale.
Then they gathered their forces near Hod in the bay
called Hjórunga,[49] and there were more than three hundred and sixty ships. Then they laid their plans.

20. PREPARATIONS FOR THE BATTLE

NOW IT IS TO BE TOLD of the Jómsvíkings that they sailed
from the south along the land, and everyone fled from
them who could. Still they killed a great many people
and made great depredations on the shore. Then they
sailed north around the promontory of Stad[50] and landed
at the Herey Islands, because they were in need of provisions. At that time they had as yet heard nothing of
Earl Hákon.

[49] Located in the district of South Möre. The description of the locale
of the battle tallies with geographical fact.
[50] The westernmost point of land on the Norway mainland.

Vagn then sailed with his galley to the island of Hod. There he encountered a man who was driving three cows and twelve goats. Vagn asked his name, and he said it was Ulf. Then Vagn said: "You men, drive this livestock down to the shore."

"Who is this man?" asked Ulf.

They told him. Then Ulf said: "It would seem to me that if you are the Jómsvíkings you could find bigger cattle for slaughter, and not far away."

Vagn said: "Tell us about the earl if you can, and you shall get back both your cows and your goats."

Ulf said: "He lay here yesterday evening with one ship behind the island in Hjórunga Bay."

Then Vagn said: "You shall go along with us and show us the way."

Ulf went aboard Vagn's ship and, together with some of the force, they sailed at once for the Herey Islands. The Jómsvíkings made ready for battle, even though Ulf made light of any resistance. Then Ulf feared that they suspected there were more ships than he had told of. He leapt overboard and swam off. Vagn seized a javelin and drove it through his middle, and thus Ulf lost his life.

Then the Jómsvíkings saw that the inlet was all covered with ships. They straightway put their fleet in battle array. Sigvaldi posted himself in the middle of the fleet, with his brother Thorkel on one side. Búi and his brother

Sigurd were stationed on the northern wing, and Vagn Ákason and Bjorn the Welshman on the southern wing.

In Hjórunga Bay a skerry lies in the middle, and north of the reef an island called Primsigned;[51] the island of Horund lies to the south.

Now the earl and his sons saw that the Jómsvíkings had lined up their ships in battle array against them. Svein, the son of Earl Hákon, together with Gudbrand from the Dales, was to engage Sigvaldi; and Stýrkar from Gymsar, Sigvaldi's brother Thorkel. Yrjarskeggi and Sigurd Steikling from Hálogaland[52] and Thorir Hart were to face Búi. Thorkel Midlong, Hallstein Kerling, and Thorkel Leira were arrayed against Sigurd Cape; Arnmód and his sons Arni and Finn, against Vagn. Earl Eric, the son of Earl Hákon, and Erling from Skuggi, together with Geirmund the White, faced Bjorn the Welshman. [Also][53] Einar the Small and Hávard from Flydruness. Earl Hákon was to hold himself in reserve and lend support wherever necessary.

There were four Icelanders in the fleet of Hákon and his sons. One was Einar,[54] the son of the Skald-maid. He

---

[51] Primsigned literally means "marked with the cross." The *prima signatio* was the religious act preliminary to baptism. Just why the name was applied to the island is not known.

[52] On the west coast of northern Norway.

[53] There is an evident lacuna in the text here.

[54] The most noted of the skalds at the court of Earl Hákon. He is the

leapt on to the landing stage and said: "To Sigvaldi I shall go, this earl gives grudgingly." And then he spoke this verse:

> "Up, to join the earl who
> adds to wolves' feast[55] boldly!
> Forth, to join his fleet and
> fight with Earl Sigvaldi!
> Nor will the wand-of-wounds'[56] strong
> wielder, when I find him—
> fast my shield to his ship I'll
> shift—reward begrudge me."

Earl Hákon saw that Einar wanted to leave him, and he asked Einar to come and talk with him. Then the earl took some precious scales which were made of burnt silver, all gilded. Two weights belonged with them, one of gold and the other of silver. On each weight was the figure of a man, and they were called "lots," and their nature was such that when the earl laid them on the scales

---

author of "Vellekla," one of the best-known skaldic poems, which celebrates the martial deeds of the earl and is prophetic of the prosperity of the country under him. For a translation of "Vellekla" see *The Skalds,* Hollander (Princeton University Press for the American-Scandinavian Foundation, 1945), chap. 5.

[55] Kenning for "carnage, battle." (A kenning is a periphrastic expression used in Old Germanic, especially Old Norse, poetry, instead of the simple name of a person or thing.)

[56] Kenning for "sword."

and said what each was to stand for, then if the one came up which he wanted to come up, the lot lying on that side stirred so that there was a tinkling.[57] The earl gave Einar these scales, and he rejoiced. Thereafter he was called Einar Tinkle-Scales.

Another skald was Vígfús, the son of Víga-Glúm. The name of a third one was Thord the Left-Handed. The fourth was Thorleif Skúma, the son of Thorkel from Dýrafirth. Thorleif Skúma got himself a root bole in the forest and burned it in the fire. This he brought along as a weapon, and he boarded the ship of Earl Eric.

The earl said: "What do you want to do with that big club?" Thorleif said:

> "In my hand I hold
> for Búi's head
> a bone-breaker,
> baleful for Sigvaldi,
> a woe for Víkings,
> a weapon for Hákon.
> If life be granted,
> most loathful will be
> this oaken club
> to untold Danes."

[57] A difficult passage in the original.

Vígfús also was on Earl Eric's ship. He took his spear and whetted it and spoke this verse:

"Fiercest fight—at home while
fondles the craven his buxom
wife—waxes apace now
Vithri's-weather—[58] awaits us.
Safe, I say, the weakling
sleeps, no trouble expecting,
warm in his wife's embraces;
we sharpen spears for battle."

21. THE BATTLE

THEREUPON THE TWO FLEETS joined battle and fought fiercely, nor was there need to goad them on. We are told that where Sigvaldi fought against Earl Hákon and Earl Svein, there it was a draw and neither party yielded

[58] Vithri was one of the many names of Ódin. His "weather" or "storm" was the battle.

ground with their ships. Also, Earl Eric proved to be a match for Vagn. But where Búi and his brother pushed the attack, they were found to deal weighty blows and it seemed better to give ground: Earl Hákon's men let their ships drift back, and Búi made a big dent in the battle array of the earls. There was much shouting and a terrific blowing of trumpets.

Earl Eric saw how affairs stood. He rowed to the spot and attacked Búi, and there arose the fiercest fighting. The earl managed to restore his battle line, but no more. Then there was heard a mighty whoop where Vagn and his ships were stationed. The earl rowed there. Vagn had made a clean sweep through the battle array and put that whole wing to flight. And when Earl Eric saw that, he laid his iron-prowed ship alongside Vagn's dragon, and then the battle began anew. And it is common report that there never was a more spirited fight. And right then Vagn and Áslák Holmskalli leapt up on the prow of Eric's iron-beaked ship, and each plowed forward on either side of the ship, clearing the deck, so that everybody fell back. Áslák wore no helmet on his bald pate, but though men struck his skull with their swords they no more harmed him than if they had hit with whalebone.[59]

[59] Áslák and Hávard are "berserkers," wild and enormously strong warriors invulnerable to ordinary weapons.

The weather was good, with hot sunshine, and many shed their clothing. Vagn and Áslák slew many a man. Then Earl Eric urged his men on with fiery words to the attack. Vígfús, the son of Víga-Glúm, seized a large, sharp-pointed anvil and flung it at Áslák's head, and the point forthwith sank into Áslák's skull and he fell down dead. But Vagn on his side of the ship waded forward, killing men savagely. Thorleif Skúma ran to attack him and hit him with his oaken club. The blow landed on Vagn's helmet and was so heavy that the helmet split. But Vagn leaned against the railing and hurled his sword at Thorleif, then forthwith leapt overboard and onto his own warship and kept on fighting furiously.

Earl Eric now withdrew his ship from the battle line, because its fore part back to the mast was almost cleared of warriors. By that time Earl Hákon had moved his whole fleet to the land. There was a lull in the fighting, and Earl Hákon and his sons all met together.

Earl Hákon said: "It seems to me that the battle is beginning to go against us. I had thought it a bad thing to have to fight these men, and so indeed it turns out. Now this will not do. We must bethink ourselves of some wise course. I shall go up on land, and you are to look after the fleet meanwhile, in case they attack."

Thereupon the earl went up on the island of Primsigned, and away into a forest, and fell on his knees[60] and prayed, looking northward. And in his prayer he called upon his patron goddess, Thorgerd Holgabrúd. But she would not hear his prayer and was wroth.[61] He offered to make her many a sacrifice, but she refused each one, and he thought his case desperate. In the end he offered her a human sacrifice, but she would not have it. At last he offered her his own seven-year-old son; and that she accepted. Then the earl put the boy in the hands of his slave Skopti,[62] and Skopti slew him.

Afterwards the earl returned to his ships and urged his men on to make renewed attack; "for I know now

[60] The author erred here; the Germanic heathen did not fall on his knees before his gods.

[61] We must suppose that the goddess's wrath was owing to Hákon's earlier temporary acceptance of Christianity.

[62] Also known as Kark; the same man who afterwards betrayed and killed the earl when he fled from Ólaf Tryggvason.

surely that the victory will be ours. Press the attack all the more vigorously, because I have invoked for victory both the sisters, Thorgerd and Irpa."

Then the earl boarded his ship and prepared for the fight, and the fleet rowed to the attack, and again there was the most furious battle. And right soon the weather began to thicken in the north and clouds covered the sky and the daylight waned. Next came flashes of lightning and thunder, and with them a violent shower.[63] The Jómsvíkings had to fight facing into the storm, and the squall was so heavy that they could hardly stand up against it. Men had cast off their clothes, earlier, because of the heat, and now it was cold. Nevertheless, no one needed to be urged on to do battle. But although the Jómsvíkings hurled stones and other missiles and threw their spears, the wind turned all their weapons back upon them, to join the shower of missiles from their enemies.

Hávard the Hewing was the first to see Thorgerd Holgabrúd in the fleet of Earl Hákon, and then many a second-sighted man saw her. And when the squall abated a little they saw that an arrow flew from every finger of the ogress, and each arrow felled a man. They told Sigvaldi, and he said: "It seems we are not fighting men alone, but still it behooves us to do our best."

[63] Such storms with a sudden drop of temperature, hail, and lightning are very rare on the west coast of Norway.

And when the storm lessened a bit Earl Hákon again invoked Thorgerd and said that he had done his utmost. And then it grew dark again with a squall, this time even stronger and worse than before. And right at the beginning of the squall Hávard the Hewing saw that two women were standing on the earl's ship, and both were doing the same thing that Thorgerd had done before.

Then Sigvaldi said: "Now I am going to flee, and let all men do so. I did not vow to fight against trolls, and it is now worse than before, as there are two ogresses."

Then he severed the hawsers that fastened his ship to the others and shouted to Búi and Vagn to flee too. Vagn cried: "Go ahead, wretch that you are." And in that tumult Thorkel Midlong leapt from his ship on to that of Búi and at once hewed at Búi—all this happened in a trice—cutting his lip and chin all the way down so that the teeth flew out of his head.

Then Búi said: "Less pleasant will it seem now for the Danish maiden to kiss me on Bornholm."

Then Búi returned the blow against Thorkel; it was slippery on the deck, so that Thorkel fell against the gunwale in trying to ward off the blow. The blow struck him in the middle, and he was cut in two against the gunwale.

At that moment Sigmund Brestisson, a great fighter, attacked Búi on his ship, and it ended with Sigmund cutting off both of Búi's hands at the wrists. Then Búi stuck the stumps into the handles of his chests and called out aloud: "Overboard all of Búi's men," and leaped overboard with the chests.

At that time Sigvaldi was drawing back from the fleet. Then Vagn spoke this verse:

> "Into danger drew us,
>   daring all, Sigvaldi:
> chapfallen, the churl now
> chases home to Denmark;
> fain would the hero fondly
> fold in his arms his leman
> whilst o'er bucklered broadside[64]
> Búi leaped, stout-hearted."

Sigvaldi had become chilled, so he took to the oars and rowed while another man steered.[65] Then Vagn hurled a spear at Sigvaldi, but it struck the man at the rudder and pinned him against the gunwale.

Thorkel the Tall at once abandoned the fight when Sigvaldi fled, and so did Sigurd Cape when Búi had leapt overboard; and both considered themselves to have lived up to their vow. They had twenty-four ships and sailed back to Denmark.

[64] Shields fastened in solid rows to the gunwale formed an additional breastwork for the warriors.

[65] In the Old North rowing was in no wise regarded as below the dignity of noble personages.

Now it is to be told of Vagn that he renewed the defence in brave fashion, and so did all his men, and all still capable of bearing arms went aboard his warship. But Earl Eric and many other chieftains attacked it, and there was a fierce fight. The end is told by the saying "one man can't stand up against many." So many of Vagn's men had fallen that hardly eighty were left, but these still defended the raised afterdeck of the warship. Then it became so dark with nightfall that no one could longer see to fight. Thereupon Earl Eric had all the rigging taken from that ship as well as from others, and he rowed away. The earl's men stood watch over the ships that night, and put up their tents, and now could boast of a great victory.

Then they weighed the hailstones on scales to see what power Thorgerd and Irpa had, and one hailstone weighed an ounce.[66]

[66] A small weight for an ogress-induced hailstone, but understandably impressive considering the rarity of hail (see note 63).

22. THE AFTERMATH

VAGN AND BJORN the Welshman discussed what measures they should take. "We have the choice," said Vagn, "of either waiting here till daybreak to be made prisoners, or of trying to reach land to do them some damage and perhaps escape after that."

Thereupon they took the mast and the sailyard, and on them the eighty men tried to escape. They got to a skerry, but by that time most of them were altogether done for, what with their wounds and the cold, and they could proceed no further. Ten men died there during the night.

When dawn broke, the earl's men began to bind up their wounds. Then they heard the twang of a bowstring, and an arrow struck Gudbrand, a kinsman of the earl's, and the shot was mortal. Thereupon they rowed out to the ships to search them, and on Búi's ship they found Hávard the Hewing still living, though both his feet were severed. He said: "Who of the men fell a while ago from my shot?" They told him.

Hávard said: "Then I was less lucky than I would like to have been. I had meant it for the earl."

Then they slew Hávard.

Earl Eric went up to Thorleif Skúma and asked: "How is it—you look as though you were at death's door?"

Thorleif said: "I don't know—except that the point of Vagn's sword touched me a bit, yesterday, when I struck him that blow with my club."

The earl said: "Ill bestead would your father be if you died." Einar Tinkle-Scales overheard this and spoke this verse:

> "Said the earl to the sea-steed's[67]
> sailor there in south-lands—
> grievous gashes marked the
> gold-dispender's[68] body—:
> woeful sorrow, ween I,
> will your father suffer
> if, urger-of-the-storm-of-
> arrows,[69] you should die now."

Then Thorleif died.

Afterwards they discovered that there were men on the skerry. So the earl bade his men go after them and capture them. They rowed out to them, and the men put

---

[67] Kenning for "ship." [68] Kenning for "chieftain."
[69] Kenning for "warrior."

up no defence. Seventy were then brought to the mainland. The earl had them all fastened in one rope. All the ships of the Jómsvíkings were towed to the land and their goods divided among the earl's men. Then the earl's men opened their provisions and ate, and there was much jubilation. And when they had eaten their fill they went to where the prisoners were.

23. THE TESTING OF THE JÓMSVÍKINGS

THORKEL LEIRA had been picked to deal the Jómsvíkings the deathblow. Then three men were released from the rope, all badly wounded, and slaves were assigned to guard them and twist wands into their hair. Then Thorkel Leira went up to them and lopped off their heads.

Afterwards he said: "Did you observe whether I changed color at all in this business?[70] For many say that happens if one kills three men."

Earl Eric said: "We did not see you change color, yet a great change seems to have come over you."

[70] The belief obtained that a change of color (or any other sign of a change visible on the face) betokened a man's being "fey"—doomed.

Thereupon a fourth man was released from the rope, and a wand was twisted in his hair. He too had been sorely wounded.

Thorkel asked him: "What do you think about dying?"

"I am resigned to it," he replied; "the same will happen to me as happened to my father."

"What was that?" asked Thorkel.

He said: "Slash away! He died."

Then Thorkel dealt him the deathblow.

Then a fifth man was brought up, and Thorkel asked him what he thought about dying.

He said: "Poorly would I remember the laws of the Jómsvíkings if I shrank from death or spoke words of fear. Death comes to every man."

Thorkel dealt him the deathblow.

Thereupon they were minded to ask the same of every man of them before he was slain and thus find out whether the band was as gallant as it was reputed to be. And the repute, they thought, would be borne out if no one spoke words of fear.

The sixth man was brought up with a wand twisted in his hair. Thorkel spoke to him in the same fashion. The man said it was well to die in high esteem with men; "but you, Thorkel, will live with shame."

Thorkel cut him down.

Then a seventh man was led there, and Thorkel asked him the question.

"I think well of dying. Just cut me down quickly. Here I hold a knife in my hand. We have often talked, we Jómsvíkings, about whether a man knows anything when he is quickly beheaded. So let this be the proof of the matter: I shall hold up this knife if I know of anything; else it will drop."

Thorkel hewed, the head flew off, and the knife dropped.

With that the eighth man was brought out, and Thorkel asked him the same question.

He said he thought well of dying. And when he thought the blow would fall he said: "Hrút [Ram]!"

Thorkel checked himself and asked why he uttered that word.

He replied: "Even so, one would not be too many for the [two] ewes you called on, you earl's men, the time you got a drubbing from us."[71]

"Wretch that you are," said Thorkel, and chopped off his head.

Upon that a ninth man was brought out, and Thorkel asked him the same question.

He said: "I think well of death, as do all of us. But I

[71] In the original a pun is involved, since á (dative and accusative of ær, "ewe") is in Icelandic the equivalent of "ouch."

am not minded to let myself be slaughtered like a sheep, and would rather face the blow. You hew into my face and watch closely if I flinch. Because we Jómsvíkings have often talked about that."

They did what he asked for and let him face the blow. Thorkel stepped in front of him and hewed into his face; and he did not flinch a whit except that his eyes closed when death came upon him.

Then the tenth man was brought up, and Thorkel put the question to him. But he replied: "I wish you would wait till I let down my trousers."

"That I shall grant you," said Thorkel.

And when the man had done his business he said: "Many a thing turns out differently from what one expected. I intended to get into bed with Thóra, the daughter of Skagi, who is the earl's wife." And he shook his member and pulled up his trousers.

Then Earl Hákon said: "Strike down that man at once, he has long had ill in his mind."

Thorkel gave him the deathblow.

Then there was brought up a young man whose hair was long and golden yellow like silk. Thorkel asked him the same question.

He said: "I have lived the best part of my life. I do not care to live after those who have died here. But I want to be led to slaughter not by slaves but rather by a man not lower than you; nor will such a one be hard to find—and let him hold my hair away from my head so that my hair will not become bloodstained."

A man from the earl's bodyguard stepped forward and wound the long hair around his hands. Thorkel slammed down with his sword, and at that moment the young man jerked away his head, and the blow fell on the arms of the one holding his hair and cut them off at the elbow.

The young man leapt up and said: "Whose hands are in my hair?"

Earl Hákon said: "A great mischief has been done. Kill that man at once and also all the others who are left, because these men are too unmanageable to guard against."

Earl Eric said: "Let us first find out who they are. What is your name, young man?"

He replied: "They call me Svein."

The earl asked: "Whose son are you?"

He said: "I am said to be the son of Búi."

The earl asked: "How old a man are you?"

He replied: "If I live through this one I shall be eighteen years."

Earl Eric said: "You shall." Then he took him into his company.

Earl Hákon said: "I do not know what will happen if

he who has done us such despite is to escape death. Yet I shall let you have your will. Now keep on beheading these men."

Then another one was released from the rope, but it caught around his foot so that he was held fast. He was a tall man, young, and of very brisk manner. Thorkel asked him what he thought of death.

"I would think well of it if I could fulfill my vow before dying."

Earl Eric said: "What is your name?"

"My name is Vagn," he replied.

The earl asked whose son he was, and he said that he was the son of Áki.

The earl said: "What is the vow that would satisfy you to fulfill before dying?"

"This," he said: "that once I got to Norway I would get into bed with Ingeborg, the daughter of Thorkel Leira, without the consent of her kinsfolk, and that I would kill Thorkel myself."

"That I shall prevent," said Thorkel as he rushed at him and leveled a blow with both hands. Bjorn the Welshman gave Vagn a kick so that he fell forward. Thorkel's blow went over Vagn's head, and he stumbled as he missed Vagn; but his sword flew out of his hands and cut the rope so that Vagn was free. Vagn leapt up and seized the sword and dealt Thorkel the deathblow.

Then Vagn said: "Now I have fulfilled half of my vow, and I feel a good deal better satisfied."

Then Earl Hákon said: "Don't let that man escape! Kill him at once."

Earl Eric said: "He shall no more be killed than I will."

Earl Hákon said: "I can do nothing about this business, since you insist on having your own way."

Earl Eric said: "Vagn will be an acquisition for us, and I hold him a great trade for Thorkel Leira."

Afterwards Earl Eric asked Vagn to come into his company.

Then Vagn said: "Only on this condition do I think it better to live than to die: that quarter is given to all our men. Else let us all go one way."

Earl Eric said: "I shall now speak to them, for I am not averse to doing what you ask."

Then he went up to Bjorn the Welshman and asked his name. Bjorn told him.

The earl said: "Are you that Bjorn who showed such prowess in rescuing the man in the hall of King Svein? And what cause had you, an old man and white-haired, to attack us? Sure it is that every man's hand is against us. Will you accept your life from us?"

Bjorn said: "I will, if quarter is given to Vagn, my foster son, as well as to all those who still live."

"That I shall grant you if I have the power."

Earl Eric then asked his father that quarter be given to all Jómvíkings who were still alive. Earl Hákon told him to do as he pleased. Thereupon all were released and assured of their lives.

24. OF VAGN, SIGVALDI, AND THE OTHER JÓMSVÍKINGS

AFTER THAT VAGN on the advice of Earl Eric journeyed east to Víken and announced that he would celebrate his marriage with Ingeborg, as had been his intention. Vagn remained there during the winter, but in spring he journeyed south to Denmark to his possessions in Funen and managed them for a long time. And many men of renown are descended from him and Ingeborg, who was considered a most outstanding woman. Bjorn journeyed home to Wales and ruled there as long as he lived, and he was considered a very admirable man.

When Sigvaldi returned home to Denmark he went to his possessions in Zealand. His wife, Ástrid, was waiting for him there. She had a bath made ready for him and rubbed him down herself. She said: "I am thinking that some who were in the Jómsvíking battle carried away from it a hide more riddled with holes than yours—yours seems to be best cared for with powder [like a woman's]."[72]

He replied: "Things might still happen to me that you might be even less pleased with; so be satisfied with things as they are."

Sigvaldi ruled over Zealand and was considered a man of exceeding shrewdness. He plays a part in several sagas. Thorkel the Tall also was held to be a very wise man, as was proved often afterwards.[73]

Sigurd Cape took over his paternal inheritance on the island of Bornholm and was considered a most worthy man. A long line of descendants stem from him and Tova.

Some men say that Búi became a dragon and brooded on his gold. Their reason for the tale was that a serpent had been seen in Hjórunga Bay; and it may be that some evil spirit did settle on that treasure and was seen there.

Earl Hákon did not rule over Norway for very long after the battle, but he was greatly renowned for the vic-

[72] Whole wheat is still used in the bath for softening the skin.
[73] Thorkel headed an expedition against England, but later, together with King Ólaf Haraldsson (better known as Saint Ólaf), entered the services of King Æthelræd against King Svein Forkbeard of Denmark.

tory. Then there came to Norway the famous King Ólaf, the son of Tryggvi, and it then happened that Earl Hákon was murdered, according to what we are told in the sagas of the kings.[74] King Ólaf then converted all of Norway. Here we cease telling about the Jómsvíkings.

[74] See note 19.